Deserts

Jane & Steve Parker

Consultant: Keith Lye

FRANKLIN WATTS
A Division of Grolier Publishing
NEW YORK • LONDON • HONG KONG • SYDNEY
DANBURY, CONNECTICUT

© Franklin Watts 1997

First American Edition 1998 by
Franklin Watts
A Division of Grolier
Publishing Co., Inc.
Sherman Turnpike
Danbury, Connecticut 06813

Library of Congress Cataloging-in-Publication Data

Parker, Jane, 1951–
　　Deserts / Jane & Steve Parker
　　　　　p.　　cm. — (Take 5 geography)
　　Includes index.
　　Summary: An overview of the rich and varied environments of the earth's desert regions as exemplified by five of the driest deserts in the world.
　　ISBN 0-531-14460-7
　　1. Deserts—Juvenile literature.　[Deserts.]　I. Parker, Steve.　II. Title.
III. Series.
GB611.2.P37　1998
551.41'5—dc21

　　　　　　　　　　　　　　　　　　　　　　　　　　　97-20772
　　　　　　　　　　　　　　　　　　　　　　　　　　　　　CIP
　　　　　　　　　　　　　　　　　　　　　　　　　　　　　　AC

Series editor: Kyla Barber
Designer: Ness Wood
Illustrator: Joanna Biggs
Picture researcher: Susan Mennell
Art director: Robert Walster
Consultant: Keith Lye

Printed in Great Britain

Photographic credits:

t=top, b=bottom, c=center, l=left, r=right
Cover photo, Robert Harding, Ron Watts
4 t, Christine Osborne Pictures, C. Barton;
4 b, Images;
5, FLPA, Mark Newman;
6, The Hutchison Library;
7 l, NHPA, Karl Switak;
7 r, Bruce Coleman, Gerald Cubitt;
8 The Hutchison Library, Robert Francis;
9 t, Christine Osborne Pictures;
9 l, Mountain Camera, John Cleare;
9 r, Mountain Camera, Colin Monteath;
10 l, Images;
10 r, Christine Osborne Pictures;
11, NHPA, ANT;
12 Planet Earth Pictures, William M Smithey, Jr;
13 l, NHPA, Anthony Bannister;
13 r, Still Pictures, Gilles Martin;
14 t, Images;
14 b, FLPA, D Hall;
15 l, Bruce Coleman, Andy Price;
15 r, Mountain Camera, John Cleare;
16, FLPA, David Hosking;
17 t, NHPA, Stephen Dalton;
17 r, NHPA, Anthony Bannister;
17 b, Mountain Camera, John Cleare;
18, The Hutchison Library, Val & Alan Wilkinson;
19 t, Christine Osborne Pictures;
19 bl, The Hutchison Library, Vanessa Boeye;
19 br, Planet Earth Pictures, John Downer;
20, Images;
21 l, Robert Harding;
21 r, Robert Harding;
22, Christine Osborne Pictures;
23 l, Still Pictures, Voltchev-Unep;
23 r, NHPA, Karl Switak;
24 t, Images;
24 b, Christine Osborne Pictures;
25 t, Christine Osborne Pictures;
25 b, Bruce Coleman, Staffan Windstrand;
26, Panos Pictures, Ron Giling;
27 t, Panos Pictures, Guy Mansfield;
27 r, NHPA, Anthony Bannister;
28 t, Colorific!, Pierre Boulat/Cosmos
28 b, NHPA, Anthony Bannister;
29 l, Still Pictures, Jorgen Schytte;
29 r, Still Pictures, Mark Edwards;
31, Planet Earth Pictures, Thomas Dressler.

Contents

What Are Deserts? 4
How Deserts Form 6
Different Deserts 8
Wind in the Desert 10
Water in the Desert 12
Adapted to Survive 14
Creatures Under the Sun 16
Desert Peoples 18
Desert Cities 20
Making the Desert Bloom 22
Leisure and Pleasure 24
Desert Wealth 26
Conserving Deserts 28

Glossary 30
Fact File 31
Index 32

What Are Deserts?

In the middle of a desert what can you see? Three Ss—sand, sky, sun. No clouds, houses, roads, trees, or life of any kind. The landscape is totally deserted, hence "desert."

However, few deserts are really so empty. Most dry, or arid, places have a variety of scenery, such as rocks, cliffs, canyons, even rivers and oases – and the world's hardiest plants and animals.

Deserts may be stony, like parts of the Sahara (above), sandy, like California's Mojave-Sonora Desert (below), or may consist of bare rock.

Largest desert

The world's biggest desert is the Sahara, in North Africa. *Sahara* means "desert" in Arabic, and it is larger than the next eight biggest deserts added together. Like all deserts, it is dry because more water is lost from the ground than falls onto it as rain, snow, or dew. The water is lost by drying—going back into the air as invisible water vapor (which is called evaporation), or by draining away deep into the soil and rocks.

Areas in square miles: **Sahara:** 3,474,900; **Gobi:** 443,900;

Take 5 deserts

Sahara: (Northern Africa) Cave paintings show it was once green and lush, but it is now the largest desert on Earth.

Gobi: (Central Asia) This is the furthest desert from the sea.

Mojave-Sonora: (North America) Home to huge cacti and the sidewinder snake, parts are now protected nature parks.

Gibson: (Australia) Plants, animals, and people fight heat and drought in this dry country.

Atacama: (Chile) This area is a barren wilderness that yields valuable salts and minerals.

Valley of the Dead

The hottest, driest, and lowest place in North America is Death Valley, California, U.S. The air temperature can rise above 131°F (55°C) in the midday sun—a hot bath is 113°F (45°C). The ground itself may reach 174°F (79°C), easily hot enough to burn through skin. Less than 2 inches (40 mm) of rainfall in a typical year. The valley is named in memory of the many pioneers who died struggling across it during the California gold rush of 1849.

Salt flats in Death Valley.

Yearly rainfall chart

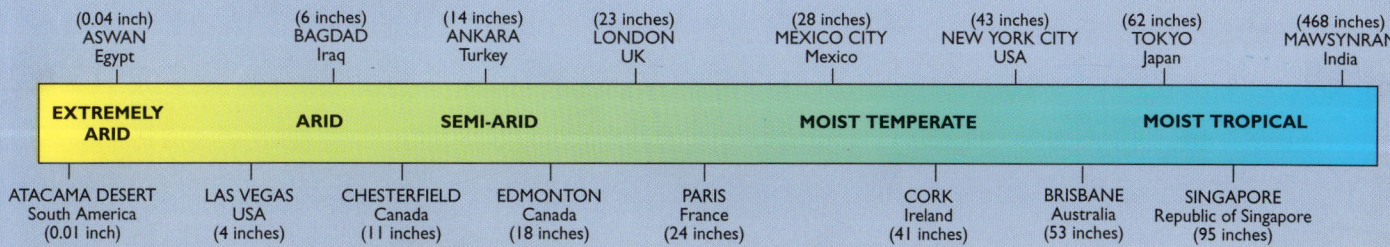

Mojave-Sonora: 135,100; **Gibson:** 115,800; **Atacama:** 54,040.

How Deserts Form

In the local language of the Mongol people, in central Asia, *Gobi* means "place without water." The Gobi Desert has hardly any water because it is in the middle of the huge Asian continent, far from the sea. But why should this make it so very dry?

In the the Gobi Desert, Mongolia, huge sand dunes tower above low-lying plains of sparse grasses, which are grazed by sheep, camels, and yaks.

Continental deserts

As air blows over the sea, it picks up moisture. Winds continue across the coast and over the land where the air cools. The water vapor in the air condenses, or turns back into drops of water or crystals of ice, and falls as dew, rain, sleet, or snow. As the winds carry on, they become drier. Far inland, they have little rain left.

Some of the sand dunes in the Gobi Desert have crests more than 328 feet (100m) high.

Whichever way the winds blow over Asia, they lose their moisture long before they reach the Gobi. So the Gobi is called a continental desert because it's in the middle of a continent. There are many other continental desert areas too, especially in Australia, Africa, Arabia, and the Americas.

Types of desert: **Gobi:** continental; **Mojave-Sonora:** rain shadow;

Tropical deserts

Deserts form in other ways, too. Warm air from the equator, around the hot middle of Earth, rises, moves north or south, and gets cooler. Its moisture condenses and falls as rain, especially over the great tropical rain forests. The air descends in regions around the tropics of Cancer and Capricorn; it is now warm and dry. In these areas, deserts may form.

Rain shadow

Winds are forced to rise as they blow over mountains, causing the moisture they carry to condense and fall as rain. By the time the winds reach the far side of the mountain, they have lost all their moisture and are now very dry. In these conditions, deserts can form in the mountain's "rainless shadow."

Death Valley formed in a rain shadow region.

Coastal deserts

Some deserts are narrow strips of land along coasts of continents. They include the Namib Desert in Africa (see page 13) and the Atacama Desert in South America. They form where cold ocean currents flow close to coasts. As moist winds blow towards the land from the oceans, over these cold currents, their temperatures fall. The moisture carried by the winds then condenses into drops, which form clouds of sea mist and fog.

By midday, the sun has burned away the coastal fog from the Namib Desert.

DIFFERENT DESERTS

Rain falls on mountains — Dry air
RAIN SHADOW DESERT

Rain falls near coast — Air becomes drier as it blows inland
CONTINENTAL DESERT

Gibson: continental; **Atacama:** coastal; **Sahara:** so big that it's all of these!

Different Deserts

Many people picture deserts as endless areas of sand, like a huge beach without the sea. In fact, only one-third of dry areas and deserts are covered with loose sand – these are called "ergs". Many are stony – known as "reg", others are covered by bare rock – and are known as "hammada". Some deserts are even icy!

The Gibson's gibbers

Australia is the world's smallest continent, and also, on average, the driest. More than half of the land is semiarid or arid, and almost one-quarter is very arid—true desert.

Australia has the three main kinds of desert landscape—erg, reg, and hammada. In the Gibson Desert continual heating and cooling cracks rocks into pieces. These roll about in the wind, and become rounded pebbles known as gibbers.

Rocks broken from the nearby hills litter the surface of the Atacama Desert.

Desert with the biggest proportion of sand: the **Sahara**, at one-quarter.

Sandy and rocky deserts

In northwest Australia is the Great Sandy Desert. As its name suggests, it is covered by windblown sand. This type of desert is called erg. The largest region of erg is the southern Arabian Desert, known as the Rub 'al Khali ("Empty Quarter"). It covers 254,760 square miles (660,000 sq km), almost as large as Texas.

In the middle of Australia, or the "Red Center", the Central Ranges are simply bare rocks, called hammada. The power of the Sun and the wind wears them into fantastic shapes.

An ice desert

Most of the great southern continent of Antarctica is a giant icy desert! There is no water at all—at least, no liquid water. It's all frozen into solid ice, and living things cannot use it, so there are none! Snowfall is also very low, about 4 to 8 inches (100 to 200mm) per year in some places. Antarctica is the coldest desert, too. During the endless winter darkness, temperatures can fall to minus 126°F (–88°C), making it the coldest place on Earth.

Most of Antarctica is ice, snow, or windswept rocks.

Hardly any plants grow in the shifting Arabian sands (above). But tough bushes and cacti survive among the rocks of the Mojave-Sonora Desert.

Badlands

Only the driest deserts are lifeless. Most have scattered, scrubby plants. In southern Australia, the Nullarbor Plain is dotted with mulga trees and spinifex grass, forming mulga bushland. In America, a similar type of rocky, semiarid landscape is known as the Badlands.

This is equivalent to more than 772,000 square miles (2 million sq km).

Wind in the Desert

Wind is a powerful force in the desert. The glaring Sun heats the ground and the air above it. Hot air rises, and cooler air rushes in to take its place, producing winds – from gentle breezes to howling gales.

Blasted by sand

Wind may clear away all the loose sand and soil from an area, leaving bare, rocky hollows and basins. It piles the sand into the hills we call dunes. It can also blow the sand along in a sandstorm, hurling it at rocks and other objects, scouring them like a giant sand-blaster. As the wind slows down, the sand settles back onto the ground, smothering huge areas.

The wind blows sand to form ridges and grooves.

Wind-blown sand undercut this rock pedestal.

Wind sculptures

Fierce, sand-laden winds create amazing natural sculptures from desert rocks. The grains erode away softer types of stone more quickly than the harder, resistant layers. The direction and speed of the winds also vary. The results are wide ridges and furrows, narrow grooves known as yardangs, tall mushroom shapes called zeugens, spires, pinnacles, arches, and many other strange and beautiful rock formations.

The largest sand dunes in the world are found in the Algerian area of the **Sahara**.

Desert dunes

The shape and size of a sand dune depends on the wind's speed and direction, and the type of landscape beneath.

1 Parabolic dunes have two crescent points, or "horns", point into the wind. Strong winds produce a "blowout area" between them where wind has scooped out sand and blown it along.

2 Transverse dunes form at right angles to steady winds.

3 Barchans are crescent-shaped dunes. They usually form where wind piles sand around plants or rocks and blows around the sides. The two horns face downwind.

4 Seifs are long dunes that form parallel to the main wind direction and are found where sand is scarce.

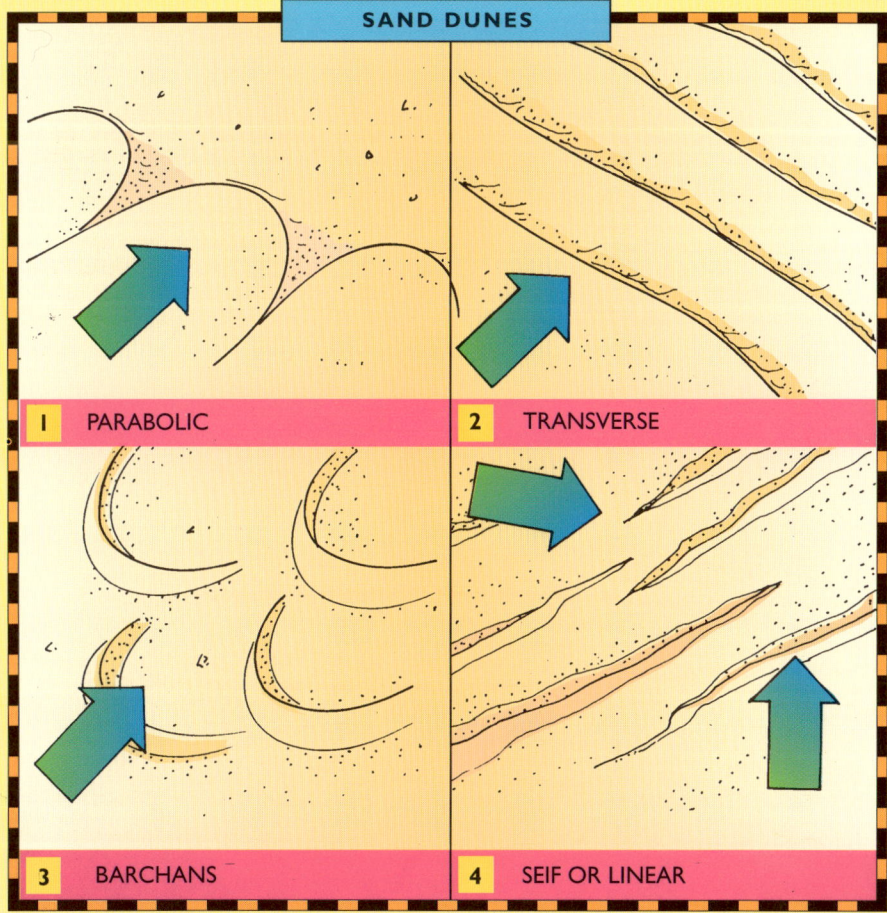

Sacred rock

Uluru, in the central desert of Australia, is the largest single, isolated rock in the world. Also called Ayers Rock, it is about 6,562 feet (2,000m) long, 4,922 feet (1,500m) wide and 1,148 feet (350m) high. As the sun moves across the sky, the rock shines with eerily changing colors. To the local Aboriginal people this is a sacred place, and their ancient rock art decorates its walls and caves.

Uluru glows in the evening sun.

They can be up to 1,640 feet (500m) high and 3,000 miles (5,000km) long.

Water in the Desert

For weeks, months, even years, conditions in the desert hardly change. Every day is hot and sunny, every night is cool and starlit.

Then, suddenly, comes the rain. Gigantic and violent storms bring huge raindrops that hammer onto the ground. Within minutes, the land is covered with sheets of gushing, flooding water and the desert landscape changes to surging floods.

Rushing floodwaters scour the desert rocks into amazing cliffs and canyons.

Water erosion

The water pours into steep-sided, flat-bottomed valleys, called arroyos or wadis. Over centuries, it has worn grooves into the rocks to form narrow, isolated flat-topped hills called buttes, and larger flat-topped areas known as mesas.

Below the Nile River, in the Sahara, flows an underground river which carries six times more water.

Each flood washes bits of sand and rock from high ground to the lowlands. As the water slows down and spreads out, the sand and rock pieces settle to form an alluvial fan. Several fans may join into wide aprons, called bahadas.

Desert rivers: **Sahara:** Nile and Niger; **Mojave-Sonora:** Mojave and Colorado;

Surface water

In addition to rain, surface water also includes hail, sleet, snow, dew around dawn and dusk, and fog or mist, especially near the sea. Most deserts have rivers too. Some may be dry for months or years. Others are more permanent, bringing much-needed water to the desert area. In North America, the Colorado River brings water from the Rocky Mountains down to the Mojave-Sonora Desert.

Some deserts have no rain, but fog.

Lost in the sands

The Okavango River flows southeast, 990 miles (1,600 km) through Angola and Botswana in Africa. But it never reaches the sea. Its waters dribble away into the sands of the Kalahari Desert, at a huge area of swampland, the Okavango Delta. Flamingos, pelicans, frogs, and other water-loving animals and birds thrive here, in the middle of the hot Kalahari.

The Okavango Delta is a huge marshy oasis in the Kalahari Desert.

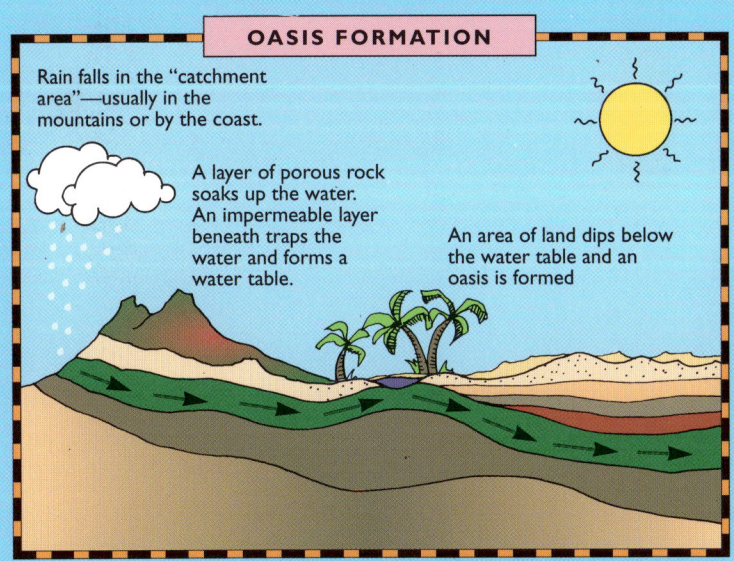

OASIS FORMATION

Rain falls in the "catchment area"—usually in the mountains or by the coast.

A layer of porous rock soaks up the water. An impermeable layer beneath traps the water and forms a water table.

An area of land dips below the water table and an oasis is formed

Rain falls on the mountainside. Water is transported through the porous rock. When the level of the land falls below the surface of the porous rock, an oasis forms.

Underground water

Some deserts have underground rivers. The Mojave River flows under the surface for much of its course. Water also seeps down into slightly spongy or porous rocks and collects above nonspongy or impermeable rocks. This forms a layer of underground water, the water table. Where the land's surface dips below the water table, it forms a surface pool—an oasis.

Gobi: Cherien; **Atacama:** Loa (not permanent); **Gibson:** no real rivers at all!

Adapted to Survive

Apart from the very driest places, there are always some plants in the desert. They have special features or adaptations that help them to survive the lack of water, poor soil, extreme temperatures and the threat from hungry and thirsty animals.

Dead above ground—but seeds and bulbs wait below.

Playing dead

In the Gobi Desert, during the long drought, there are few plants to be seen. A few tough grasses, bushes such as sage and trees such as acacias, dot the parched landscape. They survive by "playing dead." They shut down their life processes, and their leaves go brown and withered, or even fall off. Many other plants are there, but they remain hidden until it rains. Some, like poppies, survive as small seeds in the soil or under stones. Others, like desert crocuses, tulips, and lilies, remain below ground as bulbs or corms.

Bursting into life

At last, the rains come. Within a few days, the Gobi blooms. Shoots, buds, and flowers appear. Bushes sprout new leaves, or their "dead" brown ones turn green. Seeds put down roots and push up shoots. Bulbs and corms soak up water, swell, and send up stems and green leaves.

Flowers carpet the Mojave-Sonoran Desert after rain.

The world's largest cactus grows in the Mojave-Sonora Desert.

Race against time

The plants must grow, flower, and make new seeds, as quickly as possible. Soon the drought will return. So their colorful blooms cover the land. Animals take advantage of the moisture too. They feed on the leaves, petals, and nectar, and carry pollen from flower to flower so that plant seeds can be fertilized. Within a few weeks, the hot sun and strong wind dry out the ground. The desert looks brown and lifeless again.

Inedible plants

Some desert plants continue to grow during the drought. Their waxy-coated leaves prevent their losing moisture by evaporation. Their spines, prickles, and unpleasant chemicals protect against plant-eating animals. Their roots spread up to 164 feet (50m) to soak up every drop of moisture.

Baobabs have large water-storing trunks and few water-losing leaves.

Living water barrels

Cacti are famous desert plants. They thrive in the dry lands of North America, especially Mexico. Their very long roots find as much water as possible. Their stems have folded outer "skin" that can stretch as the stem swells with stored water. To prevent water loss, the leaves become sharp spines, which also stops animals eating them.

Saguaro cacti grow as big as trees!

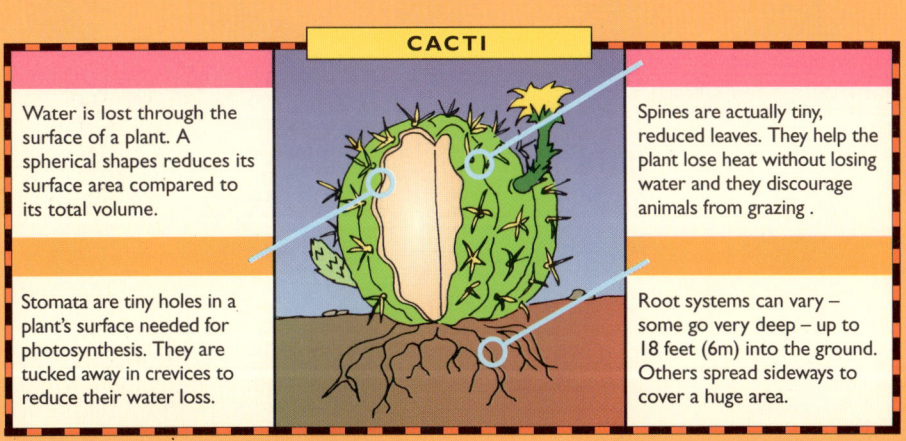

CACTI

Water is lost through the surface of a plant. A spherical shapes reduces its surface area compared to its total volume.

Stomata are tiny holes in a plant's surface needed for photosynthesis. They are tucked away in crevices to reduce their water loss.

Spines are actually tiny, reduced leaves. They help the plant lose heat without losing water and they discourage animals from grazing.

Root systems can vary – some go very deep – up to 18 feet (6m) into the ground. Others spread sideways to cover a huge area.

It is called the saguro, and it can grow up to 50 feet (15m) tall.

Creatures Under the Sun

Like desert plants, the animals who survive in the driest places have special body features and behavior. They must cope with lack of water, scarce food, and searing heat or bitter cold, as well as trying to avoid predators and finding mates for breeding.

Life on the move

One way of avoiding poor conditions is: move away! Somewhere else in the desert there may be a full oasis or puddles from recent rain. These wandering, or nomadic, creatures are usually birds or large mammals, who can cover great distances quickly, looking for food and water.

In the Gibson Desert of Australia, nomadic creatures include the wedge-tailed eagle, one of the largest eagles in the world, and the budgerigar. The budgerigar is now familiar as a cage bird, but it came originally from the dry Australian outback, where flocks of thousands of budgerigars twitter and flit between water holes.

Budgerigars, a small type of parrot, feed mainly on grass seeds.

Life underground

Another way of avoiding the heat is to hide below ground during the day. Mammals like the wombat, brown desert mouse, and spinifex-hopping mouse stay in their burrows, emerging in the cool of evening. They hardly need to drink, since they take in moisture from their food of seeds and other plant parts, and lose only tiny amounts of water in their concentrated urine and very dry droppings.

Australia's largest desert-dwellers are the red kangaroo, weighing over 176 pounds (80 kgs) and the emu, the world's second-biggest flightless bird.

Feared desert snakes: **Sahara:** saw-scaled adder; **Gobi:** mamushi (Asiatic pit viper);

A desert scorpion arches its tail, warning of its poisonous sting.

Beware the poison!

Many desert creatures—spiders, centipedes, scorpions, and snakes—have poisonous bites or stings. Prey comes past only rarely, so strong venom makes sure it will not get away. One of the Gibson Desert's strangest creatures is a spiky lizard, the "thorny devil". It looks fierce, but it is a slow-moving anteater.

Camels

Perhaps the best-known desert animals are camels. They live in Africa and Asia. Camels are also found in Australia where they are descended from the camels brought to help pioneers explore the Australian outback and to carry supplies, over 150 years ago. Like many desert dwellers, their woolly coats protect them from the sun and the cold.

Camels in the Gobi Desert must survive the freezing cold as well as the scorching heat.

Shifting sands

Desert animals have special ways of moving over hot, loose sand. To avoid being burned, the sidewinder snake throws its body forward in waves. Only two small areas of the underside touch the scorching ground at any one time. Australia's desert skink and golden mole "swim" through loose sand, as though it were water. So does the sandfish, a lizard from North Africa.

The sidewinder leaves its characteristic tracks in the sand.

Gibson: bandy-bandy; **Atacama:** snouted lance head; **Mojave-Sonora:** sidewinder.

Desert Peoples

Despite the lack of food and water in deserts and arid lands, about 700 million people live there—one-eighth of the world's population. Some scratch an existence as farmers in semiarid regions. A few are nomadic, wandering across the drier regions as they herd their animals in search of new pastures.

Among the nomads are the Tuareg of the Sahara. They keep camels, horses, goats, and cattle, and move with the seasons. With their skills and experience, they can usually find vegetation for their animals.

Ancient and independent

The Tuareg once made a living from the desert by guiding travelers through the parched Saharan wastelands. They controlled the huge camel caravans that had once carried slaves, spices, gold, ivory, and other precious cargoes along the ancient trade routes between Asia and Europe. They speak Berber, an ancient African language, and have kept their history alive by storytelling. They have wandered through many African countries, but they have stayed an independent people, with their own customs and laws.

Some Tuareg people no longer wander the Sahara. They have settled around the desert's edge, in small villages.

Average day-time temperatures: **Sahara:** 131°F (55°C); **Mojave-Sonora:** 122°F (50°C);

The Bedouin are an ancient nomadic people of north Africa and the Middle East.

Changed lifestyle

Today, goods are carried by trucks roaring along desert roads. The Sahara is divided among various African countries, with border fences and guard posts. Long droughts and failed farms make it even harder to find grazing. Many nomadic people can no longer follow their traditional lifestyle. Some have taken to a settled way of life.

Hunter-gatherers

The Kung of the Kalahari Desert still follow a traditional hunter-gatherer way of life. They speak a language that includes many clicking sounds, and their history is rich in myths and legends. They live in cool grass huts or caves decorated with beautiful paintings.

The people of the Kalahari have less homeland, as more of the desert is irrigated and farmed.

A Mongol yurt, or tent, protects against the Gobi's cool, dry winds.

Other desert dwellers

Other desert dwellers include groups of Mongols in the Gobi. They lead wandering lives, depending on their camels, yaks, goats, and sheep. In Australia, Aboriginal people can survive in the driest outback, hunting animals such as wallabies and lizards, and gathering plant food.

Gobi: 113°F (45°C); **Gibson:** 113°F (45°C); **Atacama:** 68°F (20°C)—cooled by onshore winds.

Desert Cities

Most towns and cities evolved near water. People used the water for drinking, washing, cooking, farm crops, and animals. About 5,000 years ago, ancient Egyptian people settled on the banks of the Nile. They farmed the narrow strips of fertile land between the river and the dry Sahara. The Sumerians settled in Mesopotamia, the area between the Tigris and Euphrates Rivers, on the edge of the Arabian Desert. Further east, farms and towns evolved along the Indus River in India, by the Thar Desert.

The Ancient Egyptians built the pyramids at the desert's edge.

Cradles of civilization

The Ancient Egyptians and Sumerians pushed forward the boundaries of science, technology, and art in many ways: they built towns and cities, invented machines for irrigating their crops, and developed methods of organizing society, with palaces and temples for the rulers and governments. So began the first civilizations, on the edges of the deserts.

Desert-edge cities: **Sahara:** Cairo—10 million people; **Mojave-Sonora:** Pheonix—1 million;

"City of Angels"

Cities continued to grow up on the edges of deserts. In North America, Mojave people lived between the Mojave-Sonora Desert and the Colorado River, for many centuries. Then, in the 1800s, pioneers and gold-miners arrived, forcing them to move away. One of the mining towns was given a Spanish name meaning "The Town of Our Lady, the Queen of the Angels of Porciúncula." This name was soon shortened to City of Angels—Los Angeles.

Shibam, a desert city in the Republic of Yemen, nestles in the sand. Tall, white-painted buildings help to keep out the blistering heat.

Running out of water

The Los Angeles area is now home to more than 15 million people. But it's still almost desert, with only 12 inches (30cm) of rain yearly. This is nowhere near enough water for all the people, so extra water is taken from the Colorado River or pumped up from the ground. This underground water is used up many times faster than it collects, but still "LA" grows.

Holy City in a dry land

There has been a settlement on the desert site of Jericho, now in the Israel-occupied West Bank, for at least 10,000 years. The first inhabitants were Stone Age hunters who built shelters of sun-dried mud bricks and began to farm. As more houses were built on old foundations, a mound called a tell grew up. About 7,000 years ago, the people built huge stone walls around the tell to keep out intruders. These became the "walls of Jericho," mentioned in the Bible.

Some remnants of the ancient city of Jericho still stand today.

Gobi: Ulan Bator (capital of Mongolia)—more than 1/2 million people.

Making the Desert Bloom

Could deserts help to solve the world food shortage? Some might produce food—with the right crops or farm animals and suitable watering or irrigation systems. In deserts such as the Negev, in Israel, huge glass-houses grow tomatoes, melons, and peppers. But it's very costly. To grow well, crops have four needs: sunshine, warmth, moisture, and soil. In the desert, there's plenty of sun and warmth. But soils are usually thin and poor. And, of course, water is always scarce!

Deserts are littered with failed farms.

Altering the desert

One answer is to alter the desert itself, so that its soils become more suitable for crops, by adding fertilizers and moisture. But many irrigation systems cause problems. Some use water diverted from rivers, along canals and pipes. This reduces the water available along the river's natural course, where the plants, animals, and farmland suffer. Other irrigation systems use water pumped from below the ground. But this is very expensive, and underground water supplies are slow to replenish.

After lying dormant in the dry desert soil for more than 6,000 years, some seeds are still able to grow if given water.

Typical annual rainfall (in inches): **Atacama:** less than 0.4 (10mm); **Gibson:** 1 to 2 (25-50mm);

Altering crops and animals

An alternative is to choose crops and animals that can survive in dry conditions. Trees such as acacias, baobabs, and eucalypts, and crops like jojobas and morama beans, can cope with dry soils. Hardy goats, ostriches, emus, and antelopes could be raised on dry pastureland. Could morama-bean soup and emu-burgers become popular dishes in desert regions?

Towering Saharan sand dunes threaten an irrigated oasis area in Libya.

A changed land

In 1797, the first sheep were brought to Australia. Today there are about 150 million. Along with millions of cattle, they graze the Australian outback, even around the edges of the Gibson and other deserts. However, sometimes they eat so much of the plant life that they cause the desert to spread, a process called desertification (see page 28).

Weed or crops?

Some plants that thrive in desert conditions can be used as crops, so farmers can make money. The tough yeheb nut of Somalia grows in dry, sandy soils and produces nutritious kernels, as well as animal food, firewood, and even dyes (coloring substances). Guayule, a desert shrub, produces a type of natural rubber.

The modern science of genetic engineering could alter these plants to bring better yields.

Jojoba oil, from the seeds, is used as a lubricant and for cooking.

Mojave-Sonora: 2 to 4 (50-100mm); **Sahara:** 2 to 5 (50-120mm); **Gobi:** 3 to 8 (75-200mm).

Leisure and Pleasure

Deserts seem unlikely places for industries such as leisure and tourism. But in today's world, many people want to see these harsh, lonely places for themselves, and experience the unique landscape and wildlife. Some people even seek the challenge of trekking through the desert, testing their survival skills against the heat, drought, and fierce forces of nature.

Many great historic monuments remain undisturbed in the Sahara.

Camels race for valuable prizes in the Middle East deserts.

Sandy sports

Some sports take place in desert areas. In the northern Sahara, racing horses and camels is very popular. More modern sports include cross-desert car races and sand-boarding, a combination of sledding and surfing down dunes.

Desert car rallies: Paris (France) to Dakar (Senegal) across the **Sahara**;

Desert safaris

Many adventurous people feel an urge to go deep into the desert, to see places that few others visit. Specialized tour companies organize desert safaris, in the company of experienced guides, using reliable four-wheel drive vehicles with radio backup.

Another new desert sport – sand-boarding in the Sahara.

Camels are adorned with flowers for the tourists.

Souvenirs

Thousands of tourists now visit Egypt to gaze in awe at the great pyramids and the Valley of the Kings, preserved so well in the dry conditions.

Surviving in the desert

Adventure organizations can teach people the basics of desert survival. Experienced instructors show them life-saving techniques, such as:

• Make sure that the people back at base know your route and schedule, and stay in touch by radio.

• Stay with a stranded vehicle for as long as possible. It gives shade and shelter and is easier to see during an air search.

• Make a landmark with rocks, branches, or patterns in sand, large enough to be seen from an aircraft.

• Move about only at dusk and night to avoid the sun's heat.

• Improvise a shelter and headdress to avoid sunburn and heatstroke.

• Drink only at dawn and dusk to avoid losing too much body water as sweat.

• Use simple items like a plastic bag to make a "solar still" to collect dew and other moisture.

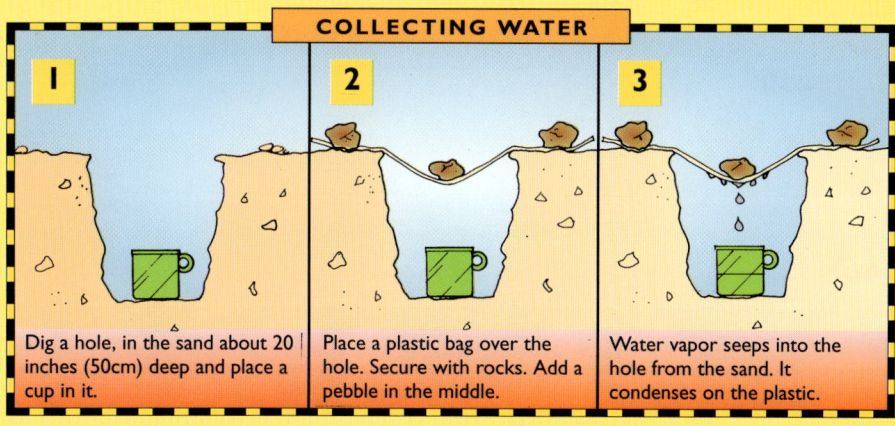

COLLECTING WATER

1. Dig a hole, in the sand about 20 inches (50cm) deep and place a cup in it.
2. Place a plastic bag over the hole. Secure with rocks. Add a pebble in the middle.
3. Water vapor seeps into the hole from the sand. It condenses on the plastic.

Collecting the morning dew using a plastic bag and a hole dug in the sand can provide vital water supplies in the desert.

Darwin to Adelaide across the Australian deserts.

Desert Wealth

There are riches in the desert. They include oil (petroleum) and rare minerals and gems such as gold, diamonds, and opals. But digging out minerals and transporting them is often hard and expensive work.

The Mojave-Sonoran Desert is part of the Great Basin. This was once the bed of the Pacific Ocean, until cut off by great earth movements and volcanoes. These caused huge changes in Earth's crust and have resulted in the region being rich in precious metals, and other minerals.

Precious metals

Gold was mined in the Great Basin area by the Aztecs, starting in the 14th century. Spanish people arrived in the 16th century, lured by tales of fabulous riches. In the 19th century, Europeans swarmed over the area in a great gold rush. Today, mining for special metals such as tungsten and chromium, as well as the traditional silver and gold, is a major industry.

Salty chemicals

When the Great Basin was cut off from the Pacific Ocean, millions of years ago, the trapped seawater slowly evaporated. It left thick layers of salts and minerals. Rain washing down from the surrounding hills brought more. Minerals such as borax, potash, and rock salt are valuable resources.

Deep beds of salt, once in prehistoric seas, cover areas in the Atacama, Mojave-Sonora and North African deserts.

Desert metal resources : **Sahara:** iron, copper, uranium, manganese; **Gobi:** few known reserves;

A new car gleams in front of an oil storage facility in Kuwait. The oil fields of the Arabian Desert bring in vast amounts of money and power—oil is a resource that most of the industrialized world relies upon.

The desert's oil

Today, most permanent settlements in the world's driest deserts are there for one reason—oil. This is so vital for our modern world that oil companies spend vast amounts of money searching for new supplies below the ground. They also spend money trying to make life more comfortable for the workers in these hot, dry places. Some of the world's largest oil fields are below the deserts of the Middle East. The countries that own them have become fabulously rich.

At the current rate of use, the reserves of oil under the deserts of the Middle East may last only 60 to 80 years.

Diamonds in the desert

Precious gemstones, like diamonds, are formed where rocks have been heated and squeezed at tremendous pressure deep within the Earth. In Southern Africa, most diamonds are mined from rocks deep underground. But in the Namib Desert, diamonds occur at the surface. As rocks erode, the diamonds fall out and are washed into streams. "Panning" the gravel in the streambed involves swirling it around in pans of water, to separate the gems from the worthless bits of rock.

Lucky find! A diamond glistens among streambed gravels.

Mojave-Sonora: silver, tungsten, gold, lead; **Gibson:** few known reserves; **Atacama:** copper.

Conserving Deserts

The remoteness of desert areas helps to protect the plants and animals that live there. Even so, there are threats. These include mining and oil drilling, pipelines, and cross-desert roads, which bring refueling stops, hotels, and shanty towns.

Desertification

Desert areas have grown and shrunk over millions of years, as the world's climate slowly changes. This natural process is called desertization.

Discarded cans litter the Sahara in this part of Algeria.

But today there is also desertification. People try to grow crops or raise animals in the poor soil around the edges of deserts. The soil soon becomes thin and dry, and the plants die. Without their roots to hold it in place, the soil blows away. The result is a dusty, desertlike landscape, but it is an unnatural habitat, where even the usual desert wildlife cannot survive.

Planting suitable trees can help to stop the desert's spread.

A pool of water in the desert may not be there at all. It may be a mirage.

Small fences help to stop the sandy soil from blowing away, so that plant roots can gain a hold.

"Desert" is perhaps the only major type of habitat that is increasing, due to both desertization and desertification

Who cares about deserts?

Both fertile land and natural desert are being destroyed by desertification. It threatens tens of millions of people, in more than 100 countries. The Atacama Desert in Chile grows by the area of ten soccer fields every day. The southern boundary of the Sahara Desert has advanced by 386,000 square miles (1 million sq km) in the last fifty years. That's over 100 acres (40 hectares) per day. But the people who are affected are usually the poor. They have little power or influence. Their problems can be ignored by the wealthy and powerful.

Electricity from the desert

One possible use for desert areas is to make solar power. The energy in the sun's light or heat is converted into electricity. Solar cells are electronic devices that change sunlight directly to electricity. In a solar furnace, hundreds of mirrors and lenses focus the sun's heat onto a boiler of water. The steam drives turbines to generate electricity. There are solar power stations in such desert areas as California, the Middle East, and Australia.

On the edge of the Sahara, a communal television runs on electricity generated from sunlight by solar cells.

A mirage is an optical illusion, caused by hot air reflecting the light.

Glossary

arid Dry. In terms of climate, an arid area usually receives an average of between 4 and 10 inches (100 and 250mm) of rainfall (including snow, hail, dew, and other forms of moisture) each year.

condense The turning of a gas or vapor into a liquid, usually because it cools. Water vapor condenses into liquid water.

continent A major landmass on Earth's surface, such as North America or Asia.

deposit Substances or minerals that have fallen or settled out, as when sand grains sink to a riverbed, or salt grains settle on a seabed.

desert A dry area with few plants or animals. In terms of climate, a true desert or very arid area usually receives less than 4 inches (100mm) of rain, snow, hail, dew, and other forms of moisture each year.

desertification The unnatural or man-made process by which areas of land become dry and turn into desertlike landscape, usually because of too much crop growing, animal grazing, and other poor farming methods.

desertization The natural process by which areas of land become dry and turn into desert, usually because the climate gradually becomes drier.

dew Droplets of water that form when water vapor in the air condenses onto a cool surface, usually in the early morning.

dissolve To mix a solid substance, such as salt or sugar, into a liquid, such as water, so it becomes part of that liquid.

dune A mound or hill, usually made of sand.

erosion Gradual breaking down and wearing away of rocks or other substances.

evaporate The turning of a liquid into a gas or vapor, usually due to heating.

fertile In relation to soils, those that contain lots of nourishment and moisture, so that plants grow well.

habitat Certain type of surroundings with characteristic plants and animals, such as a river, woodland, or mountaintop.

impermeable A substance that is hard and nonspongy, so water cannot soak into or through it.

irrigation Providing water, usually for plants to grow. It can be a natural process or man-made, as by waterwheels, pumps, ditches, or pipes.

leeward Downwind or out of the wind, relatively sheltered from the wind (see windward).

minerals Natural substances, often formed as crystals, which make up Earth's rocks. There are more than 3,000 types.

moisture Water in its various forms, such as droplets of fog, mist, or dew, or water spread through the soil and *permeable* rocks.

nomad A person who has a wandering or nomadic lifestyle, with no permanent home.

oasis A pool, pond, or well of water in a dry area.

outback An Australian term for the countryside away from the coast, in the interior—which, in Australia, is mostly scrub, bush, or desert.

permeable A substance that is spongy or porous, so water can soak into or through it.

rain-shadow Area where rain rarely falls, because it is shielded from rain-bearing winds, usually by mountains.

salt A type of mineral, sodium chloride, commonly known as rock salt, sea salt, and table salt. It consists of tiny white grains or crystals that dissolve easily in water. As seawater dries or evaporates, it leaves salt deposits.

semiarid Fairly dry. In terms of climate, a semiarid area usually receives 10 to 20 inches (250 to 500mm) of rain, snow, hail, dew, and other forms of moisture each year.

tropical In the belt of land and sea around Earth's middle, to either side of the equator, where the climate is mostly hot and damp.

water vapor Moisture, such as mist, suspended in the air, formed when water gets warm and evaporates.

windward Upwind, in the wind or exposed to the wind, and so relatively unsheltered (see leeward).

Fact File

The 20 biggest deserts in the world
approximate areas in thousands of square kilometres

NAME	REGION	AREA sq miles	sq km
Sahara	North Africa	3,475	9,000
Arabian	Middle East	888	2,300
Gobi	Central Asia	444	1,150
Patagonian	Argentina, S. America	259	670
Great Victoria	Southwest Australia	251	650
Chihuahuan	Mexico	174	450
Great Sandy	Northwest Australia	154	400
Mojave-Sonora	North America	135	350
Gibson	Western Australia	116	300
Kyzyl Kum	Kazakhstan	116	300
Taklimakan	Northwest China	104	270
Kalahari	Southwest Africa	100	260
Kara Kum	Turkmenistan	100	260
Kavir	Iran	100	260
Syrian	Middle East	100	260
Nubian	Sudan, Africa	100	260
Thar	India-Pakistan	77	200
Namib	Southwest Africa	66	170
Ust'-Urt	Kazakhstan	62	160
Atacama	Chile, S. America	54	140

Driest continent
In proportion to its size, Australia has the largest area of dry and desert land, with more than half being arid or very arid (true desert).

Lowest rainfall
Parts of the Atacama Desert in Chile, where the average rainfall is 0.004 inch (0.1mm) each year.

Longest drought
Parts of the Atacama Desert have received no rain for over 50 years.

Highest desert temperatures
Recorded in the Sahara Desert at Al'Aziz-iyah, Libya, 136°F (58°C) in 1922.

Very hot places
Dallol, Ethiopia, on the southeast edge of the Sahara, with an average of 91–93°F (33-34°C) year after year.
Death Valley, California, where it has been more than 113°F (45°C) for four weeks at a time.
Marble Bar, Western Australia, on the edges of the Gibson and Great Sandy Deserts, where it has been more than 95°F (35°C) for four months at a time.

Furthest from the sea
The Dzungaria region in China, on the western edge of the Gobi, is further from the sea—1,646 miles (2,650km)—than any other area of land on Earth.

Deserts in prehistory
During the Triassic period, 245 to 210 million years ago, much of the world's land was dry and desertlike. The first dinosaurs and mammals appeared during this time.

Today's main deserts began to form about 15 million years ago, toward the end of the Tertiary period.

Most of the present deserts were established over 3 million years ago, although their rainfalls and sizes have altered with changes in the Earth's climate.

A traffic sign in Namibia seems to state the obvious!

Index

Aboriginal people 11, 19
Africa 4, 6, 7, 13, 17, 18, 19, 24, 27
animals 4, 6, 13, 14, 15, 16-17, 18, 19, 20, 22, 23, 28
Antarctica 9
Arabian Desert 9, 20, 28
Asia 6, 8, 17, 18
Atacama Desert 5, 7, 8, 13, 15, 17, 19, 21, 23, 27, 29
Australia 6, 8, 9, 11, 16, 17, 19, 23, 25, 29

Badlands 9, 24
Berber 18
birds 13, 16, 17, 23

cacti 9, 15
California 4, 5, 29
camels 6, 17, 18, 19, 24, 25
Colorado River 12, 13, 21
crops 20, 22-23, 28

Death Valley 5, 7, 13
desert peoples 18-19
desertification 23, 28
deserts, types of 6, 7, 8
dew 4, 6, 13, 25
diamonds 26, 27
droughts 14, 15, 19, 24

Egyptians, Ancient 20, 24
erg 8, 9
erosion 10, 12
evaporation 4, 15, 26

farming 18, 19, 20, 21, 22, 23
fog 7, 13
food 18, 22

Gibson Desert 5, 7, 8, 13, 15, 16, 17, 19, 23, 27
Gobi Desert 4, 5, 6, 13, 14, 16, 19, 21, 22, 24, 26
gold 5, 18, 21, 26
Great Basin 26
Great Sandy Desert 9

hail 13
hammada 8, 9

ice 9
industry 24, 26-27
irrigation 20, 22

Kalahari Desert 13, 19
!Kung 19

languages 6, 18, 19
living in deserts 18-19, 20-21

metals 26-27
Mexico 7, 15
Middle East 24, 27, 29
minerals 26-27
mining 28
mist 7, 13
Mojave River 13
Mojave-Sonora Desert 4, 5, 6, 9, 12, 13, 14, 15, 17, 18, 21, 23, 27
Mongol people 6, 19

Namib Desert 7, 27
Negev Desert 22
Niger, River 12
Nile, River 12, 20
nomads 18
North America 5, 6, 9, 13, 15, 21, 24

oases 4, 13, 16

Okavango River 13, 16
oil 26-27, 28

plants 4, 6, 9, 14-15, 16, 19, 22, 23, 28

rain 4, 5, 6, 7, 12, 13, 14, 16, 21
rainshadow 7
reg 8
rivers 4, 12, 13, 20, 22
roads 19, 28
rocks 4, 8, 9, 10, 11, 12, 27
Rocky Mountains 13

Sahara Desert 4, 5, 7, 8, 10, 12, 14, 16, 18, 19, 20, 22, 24, 25, 26, 27, 29
sand 8, 9, 10, 12, 13
sand dunes 6, 8, 10, 11, 23, 25
sandstorm 10
sea 6, 13
sleet 6, 13
snakes 16, 17
snow 6, 7, 9, 13
soil 4, 10, 14, 22, 23, 28, 29
solar power 29
South America 6, 7, 24
sun 8, 9, 10, 11, 15, 22, 29
surviving in deserts 14-15, 16-17, 25; *see also* living in deserts

temperatures 5, 9, 14, 16
Thar Desert 22
tourism 24-25
transport 17, 18, 19
Tuaregs 18, 19

water 4, 9, 12-13, 14, 15, 16, 18, 20, 21, 22
water vapor 4, 6
wind 6, 7, 8, 9, 10-11, 15, 19